# THE GENTLE PACE

Mastering Slow Productivity for Lasting Success and Well-being

## MARIE T. CARL

Copyright © 2024 by Marie T. Carl and

All rights reserved.

No portion of this book may be reproduced in any form without written permission from the publisher or author, except as permitted by U.S. copyright law.

## Table of Contents

| Title | Pages |
|---|---|
| Introduction | 5 |
| **Chapter One: The Origin of Slow Productivity** | **17** |
| Exploring Ancient Wisdom and Cultural Practices | 17 |
| **Chapter Two: Breaking the Chains of Busyness** | **24** |
| Questioning Societal Norms | 23 |
| Rethinking Success Beyond a Full Schedule | 33 |
| **Chapter Three: Embracing the Power of Rest** | **38** |
| The Science of Restorative Practices | 42 |

Integrating Mindfulness into Daily Routines　56

Developing Awareness of Actions and Priorities　60

**Chapter Four: Key Principles of Slow Productivity**　**64**

Doing Fewer Things with Greater Intention　70

The Importance of Rest and Recovery　77

**Chapter Five: A More Sustainable Alternative**　**81**

The Pitfalls of Hustle Culture　81

Step-by-Step Advice for a Slower, More Humane Alternative　89

The Role of Slow Productivity in Sustainable

Success 95

Practices for Cultivating

Sustainable Success and Well-being 97

**Conclusion** **103**

## Introduction

In a world that thrives on the rhythm of urgency, where productivity is measured in the relentless ticking of the clock and success seems synonymous with perpetual motion, "The Gentle Pace: Mastering Slow Productivity for Lasting Success and Well-being" emerges as a soothing melody, an harmonious counterpoint to the frenetic pace of modern life.

This book is an exploration, an invitation to pause and reconsider the very essence of accomplishment. It extends an olive branch to those caught in the whirlwind of busyness, beckoning them to embrace a slower, more intentional approach to productivity. The pages that follow are not a prescription but a journey, a journey into the heart of slow productivity, a journey toward lasting success, and a journey that intertwines accomplishment with the fundamental well-being of the individual.

In the opening verses of this narrative, we find ourselves at the intersection of the modern dilemma. The world around us propels us forward with a fervor, an unyielding pressure to keep pace with the ever-accelerating demands of productivity. It's a culture that lauds the incessant pursuit of more and more tasks completed, more goals achieved, and more accomplishments to showcase. However, in this pursuit of "more," what often remains obscured is the toll it exacts on our well-being, the sacrifices made at the altar of relentless productivity.

As we traverse the first pages, the essence of slow productivity unveils itself. This is not a revolutionary concept; rather, it's a reclamation of wisdom that echoes through the corridors of time. From the serene gardens of ancient Japan to the philosophical musings of ancient Greece, slow productivity draws inspiration from traditions that understood the value of a measured, intentional pace. The Japanese concept of "Ma" speaks to the importance of space and pause, while the Greek philosophy of "Sofrosyne" advocates for balance and harmony in one's approach to life.

With each turn of the page, the narrative weaves through the labyrinth of busyness, unraveling the chains that bind us to a culture that glorifies constant activity. "The Gentle Pace" challenges the prevailing notion that success is synonymous with a perpetually full schedule. It encourages us to question the societal norms that equate busyness with achievement, beckoning us to a more profound understanding of success, one that transcends mere productivity metrics.

Rest, often overlooked in the race for success, becomes a pivotal focal point. The book delves into the science of restorative practices, unveiling the transformative power of mindfulness, meditation, and quality sleep. Here, rest is not seen as a concession to fatigue but as a strategic component in the pursuit of sustained success and well-being. It is an exploration of the nuanced dance between effort and rejuvenation, as well as productivity, and restoration.

Transitioning from theory to practice, the journey continues into the realm of mindful productivity. The narrative becomes a guide, offering practical insights and actionable strategies for cultivating a mindful approach to daily tasks. By developing a heightened awareness of actions, priorities, and the present moment, the book unveils a path toward a more intentional and purposeful engagement with productivity.

Key principles of slow productivity emerge, like beacons guiding us through the fog of constant motion. Doing fewer things with greater intention becomes a mantra, and working at a natural pace becomes an antidote to the artificial urgency imposed by the modern world. These principles become foundational stones in the construction of a new paradigm, an approach to productivity that aligns with our intrinsic nature and fosters a sense of fulfillment.

As we navigate the challenges inherent in embracing a slower pace, the book becomes a companion, offering strategies to overcome the resistance embedded in a culture that often glorifies speed. It becomes a source of resilience in the face of workplace pressures, societal expectations, and ingrained habits that resist the shift toward a more deliberate, measured approach to life.

## Setting the Scene: The Modern Dilemma

In the bustling landscape of the 21st century, where every moment seems to be consumed by the relentless pursuit of productivity and success, we find ourselves entangled in a paradoxical predicament. Despite the advancements in technology and the myriad of opportunities at our fingertips, many of us find ourselves feeling overwhelmed, stressed, and perpetually chasing after an elusive sense of fulfillment. The modern dilemma, it seems, lies not in the scarcity of resources or opportunities, but rather in the abundance of choices and the ceaseless demand for our attention and energy.

## Understanding the Pitfalls of the Fast-Paced Culture

In our quest for productivity, we have unwittingly become victims of a culture that glorifies speed and efficiency above all else. We measure our worth by the number of tasks we can accomplish in a day, the length of our to-do lists, and the speed at which we can respond to emails and messages. However, in our relentless pursuit of success, we often overlook the toll it takes on our mental, emotional, and physical well-being. The constant pressure to do more, faster, has left many of us feeling depleted, disconnected, and disillusioned.

**The Need for a Gentle Pace in Productivity**

Amidst the chaos of modern life, there emerges a quiet yet powerful antidote: the gentle pace. Unlike the frantic rush of fast-paced living, the gentle pace advocates for a more mindful and deliberate approach to productivity, one that prioritizes quality over quantity, presence over speed, and sustainability over short-term gains. It is about embracing the art of slowing down in a world that seems to be constantly speeding up, and finding harmony amidst the chaos.

It's time to break free from the tyranny of busyness and reclaim control over your time and your life. Join me on this transformative journey as we embrace the gentle pace and rediscover the joy of slow productivity for lasting success and well-being.

Are you prepared to venture out towards a more adjusted and satisfying life?

Then let us delve into it. The path may be gentle, but the rewards are profound.

## Chapter One: The Origin of Slow Productivity

In our modern world, the concept of slow productivity may seem like a novel idea, but its roots actually trace back through the annals of history. To truly understand the essence of slow productivity, it's essential to delve into its origins and explore how various cultures and civilizations have embraced this philosophy throughout the ages.

### Exploring Ancient Wisdom and Cultural Practices

Ancient civilizations across the globe recognized the importance of balance, harmony, and rhythm in their daily lives.

From the ancient Greeks to the indigenous peoples of the Americas, there existed a deep understanding of the interconnectedness of all things and the need to cultivate a sense of equilibrium in one's actions.

In ancient China, the concept of "wu wei," or effortless action, was central to Taoist philosophy. Rather than exerting force or striving for constant achievement, the Taoists advocated for a more natural and spontaneous approach to life. By aligning oneself with the flow of the universe, one could achieve greater efficiency and effectiveness in all endeavors.

Similarly, the practice of mindfulness and meditation has been a cornerstone of spiritual traditions such as Buddhism and Hinduism for thousands of years. By cultivating present-moment awareness and inner stillness, practitioners were able to tap into a deep reservoir of wisdom and insight, leading to greater clarity and focus in their daily activities.

In the West, the ancient Greeks embraced the concept of "sophrosyne," or self-control, as a fundamental virtue. Rather than giving in to excess or impulsivity, the Greeks believed in moderation and temperance in all things. By exercising restraint and discipline, individuals could achieve a state of inner balance and harmony, leading to lasting success and well-being.

## Japanese Concept of "Ma" and Greek Philosophy of "Sofrosyne"

In Japan, the concept of "ma" holds a special significance in both artistic and everyday contexts. Loosely translated as "negative space" or "interval," ma refers to the pause or emptiness between objects or events. In traditional Japanese aesthetics, ma is considered essential for creating balance, harmony, and a sense of tranquility in art and design.

In the realm of productivity, the concept of 'ma' encourages us to embrace moments of stillness and reflection amidst the busyness of daily life. By allowing for space and silence, we can cultivate a sense of clarity and perspective, enabling us to make more informed decisions and take deliberate action.

Similarly, the Greek philosophy of sophrosyne emphasizes the importance of self-mastery and moderation in achieving lasting success and well-being. Rather than being driven by external desires or societal pressures, individuals are encouraged to cultivate inner strength and resilience through the practice of self-awareness and self-control.

By integrating these ancient wisdom traditions into our modern lives, we can cultivate a more balanced and sustainable approach to productivity. Instead of being swept away by the frantic pace of modern life, we can learn to embrace the gentle rhythm of slow productivity, allowing for greater creativity, fulfillment, and well-being in all aspects of our lives.

In the chapters to come, we will delve deeper into the principles and practices of slow productivity, exploring practical strategies for incorporating mindfulness, intentionality, and self-care into our daily routines. Together, let us embark on this journey towards mastering slow productivity for lasting success and well-being.

## Chapter Two: Breaking the Chains of Busyness

In today's fast-paced world, busyness has become a badge of honor, a symbol of productivity and success. From the moment we wake up until the moment we fall asleep, our days are filled with a seemingly endless stream of tasks, obligations, and distractions. But amidst the hustle and bustle of modern life, we often lose sight of what truly matters and find ourselves trapped in a cycle of busyness that leaves us feeling exhausted, overwhelmed, and unfulfilled.

Breaking free from the chains of busyness requires a shift in mindset and a willingness to challenge the status quo. It requires us to question the pervasive belief that being busy equates to being productive and to recognize that true productivity is not measured by the number of tasks we accomplish, but by the impact and significance of our actions.

One of the first steps in breaking the chains of busyness is to cultivate awareness of our own patterns and habits. We must take a step back and examine how we spend our time, energy, and attention, and identify areas where we may be caught in the trap of busyness. Are we constantly multitasking, trying to juggle multiple tasks at once? Do we feel guilty when we're not being productive, even during moments of rest and relaxation? By shining a light on these unconscious behaviors, we can begin to reclaim control over our time and our lives.

Once we've identified the ways in which busyness manifests in our lives, the next step is to prioritize what truly matters. This requires us to distinguish between the urgent and the important and to focus our efforts on activities that align with our values, goals, and aspirations.

By saying no to non-essential tasks and commitments, we create space for the things that bring us joy, fulfillment, and meaning.

But breaking the chains of busyness is not just about saying no to external demands, it's also about saying yes to ourselves. It's about making time for self-care, rest, and rejuvenation, and honoring our need for downtime and reflection. In a culture that values constant productivity and achievement, self-care is often seen as a luxury rather than a necessity. But the truth is, self-care is essential for our physical, mental, and emotional well-being, and it's only by prioritizing our own needs that we can show up fully and authentically in all areas of our lives.

Ultimately, breaking the chains of busyness is about reclaiming our time, our energy, and our sense of agency in a world that often feels overwhelming and chaotic. It's about recognizing that we have the power to choose how we spend our days, and that true productivity lies not in doing more, but in doing what matters most.

**Questioning Societal Norms**

From a young age, we are conditioned to believe that success is synonymous with busyness, that in order to achieve our goals and fulfill our potential, we must constantly be on the go, hustling and grinding our way to the top. But what if this relentless pursuit of success is actually holding us back, keeping us trapped in a cycle of stress, burnout, and dissatisfaction?

Questioning societal norms requires us to challenge the deeply ingrained beliefs and expectations that shape our behavior and attitudes toward work, productivity, and success. It requires us to ask ourselves: What does success truly mean to me? Am I pursuing my own definition of success, or am I simply trying to live up to the expectations of others?

One of the most pervasive societal norms we must question is the cult of busyness, the idea that our worth is tied to our productivity and our ability to constantly be in motion. This belief is perpetuated by a culture that glorifies long hours and endless hustle, equating busyness with importance and status. But the reality is, that busyness does not equate to productivity, and it certainly does not equate to fulfillment.

By questioning the cult of busyness, we can begin to redefine our relationship with work and success. Instead of measuring our worth by the number of hours we work or the size of our paycheck, we can shift our focus to what truly matters to us—whether that's spending time with loved ones, pursuing creative passions, or simply enjoying the present moment.

Another societal norm we must question is the idea that success is linear, that it follows a predictable trajectory of climbing the corporate ladder, accumulating wealth and possessions, and achieving external markers of status and prestige. This narrow definition of success fails to take into account the diversity of human experience and the myriad paths to fulfillment and well-being.

Redefining success requires us to broaden our perspective and embrace a more holistic approach to life. It requires us to consider not just our professional accomplishments, but also our relationships, our health, and our overall sense of happiness and fulfillment. Success, in its truest sense, is not about reaching a destination, but about the journey itself, about embracing the ups and downs, the twists and turns, and finding meaning and purpose in every moment.

As we question societal norms and redefine our relationship with success, we open ourselves up to new possibilities and opportunities for growth and transformation. We free ourselves from the confines of convention and pave the way for a more authentic, fulfilling, and meaningful life.

## Rethinking Success Beyond a Full Schedule

In our modern world, success is often equated with busyness, with having a full schedule, a packed calendar, and a never-ending to-do list. But what if this relentless pursuit of productivity is actually hindering our ability to achieve true success and well-being? What if success lies not in doing more, but in doing less, and doing it well?

Rethinking success beyond a full schedule requires us to challenge the prevailing notion that our worth is tied to our productivity and our ability to constantly be in motion. It requires us to question the belief that success is measured by external markers such as wealth, status, and accomplishments, and to recognize that true success is ultimately a deeply personal and subjective experience.

At its core, success is about fulfillment, it's about living a life that aligns with our values, passions, and aspirations. It's about feeling a sense of purpose and meaning in our work, our relationships, and our contributions to the world. It's about cultivating a sense of balance and well-being that allows us to thrive in all aspects of our lives.

But in order to redefine success, we must first let go of the myth of the "hustle culture", the idea that we must constantly be grinding and striving in order to achieve our goals. This toxic mindset not only leads to burnout and exhaustion but also perpetuates the belief that our worth is contingent upon our productivity and our ability to constantly be in motion.

Instead of succumbing to the pressure to constantly be busy, we must learn to prioritize what truly matters and focus our energy on activities that bring us joy, fulfillment, and meaning. This may mean saying no to non-essential tasks and commitments, setting boundaries around our time and energy, and embracing the power of rest and rejuvenation.

Rethinking success also requires us to cultivate a deeper awareness of our own values, priorities, and goals. By taking the time to reflect on what truly matters to us, we can align our actions and decisions with our authentic selves, rather than trying to live up to the expectations of others.

Ultimately, rethinking success beyond a full schedule is about embracing a more holistic and sustainable approach to life. It's about finding balance and harmony amidst the chaos of modern living and prioritizing our well-being and happiness above all else. By letting go of the need to constantly be busy, we create space for what truly matters, allowing us to live more deeply, fully, and authentically.

## Chapter Three: Embracing the Power of Rest

In our fast-paced society, rest is often seen as a luxury, a reward to be indulged in only after we've completed our endless list of tasks and obligations. But the truth is, rest is not just a luxury, it's a fundamental human need, essential for our physical, mental, and emotional well-being. In this chapter, we will explore the power of rest and why it's so important to prioritize rest in our lives.

Rest comes in many forms, including physical rest, mental rest, and emotional rest. Physical rest involves giving our bodies time to relax and recharge, whether through sleep, relaxation techniques, or simply taking a break from physical activity. Mental rest, on the other hand, involves giving our minds a break from the constant barrage of thoughts and stimuli, allowing for moments of stillness and clarity. And emotional rest involves giving ourselves permission to step back from our emotions and take care of our inner selves.

One of the most important benefits of rest is its ability to replenish our energy reserves and restore our mental and emotional well-being. When we're constantly pushing ourselves to the brink of exhaustion, we deplete our energy stores and leave ourselves vulnerable to burnout, stress, and illness. But by prioritizing rest and giving ourselves the time and space to recharge, we can prevent burnout and maintain a sense of balance and harmony in our lives.

Rest also plays a crucial role in supporting our cognitive function and creativity. When we're well-rested, our brains are better able to focus, problem-solve, and think creatively. We're able to approach challenges with a clear mind and a fresh perspective, leading to more innovative solutions and better outcomes. In fact, some of history's greatest discoveries and inventions have come about as a result of moments of rest and relaxation.

But perhaps most importantly, rest is essential for our overall health and well-being. Research has shown that chronic sleep deprivation and stress can have serious consequences for our physical health, increasing our risk of heart disease, obesity, diabetes, and other chronic illnesses. By prioritizing rest and making sleep a priority, we can protect our health and reduce our risk of illness and disease.

In today's fast-paced world, it can be tempting to push ourselves to the limit in pursuit of success and achievement. But by embracing the power of rest and making time for relaxation and rejuvenation, we can cultivate a more balanced and fulfilling life. So let us not underestimate the importance of rest, for it is through rest that we find renewal, vitality, and lasting well-being.

**The Science of Restorative Practices**

In recent years, scientists have begun to uncover the profound effects of restorative practices on our physical, mental, and emotional well-being. From the benefits of sleep on memory and cognitive function to the healing effects of meditation on stress and anxiety, research has shown that restorative practices can have a transformative impact on our lives.

One of the most well-studied restorative practices is sleep. During sleep, our bodies undergo a process of repair and regeneration, allowing us to recover from the physical and mental demands of the day. Research has shown that sleep plays a crucial role in memory consolidation, learning, and cognitive function, with even short periods of sleep deprivation having a negative impact on our ability to think clearly and make decisions.

However, the quality of sleep is as important as the quantity. Deep, restorative sleep is essential for our overall health and well-being, allowing our bodies to repair themselves and our minds to recharge. By prioritizing good sleep hygiene and creating a relaxing bedtime routine, we can improve the quality of our sleep and reap the benefits of a well-rested mind and body.

Another restorative practice that has gained popularity in recent years is mindfulness meditation. Mindfulness meditation involves paying attention to the present moment with openness, curiosity, and acceptance and has been shown to reduce stress, anxiety, and depression, and improve overall well-being. By practicing mindfulness meditation regularly, we can cultivate a greater sense of peace, clarity, and resilience in the face of life's challenges.

In addition to sleep and mindfulness meditation, there are a variety of other restorative practices that can support our health and well-being. These may include activities such as yoga, tai chi, deep breathing exercises, and spending time in nature. Each of these practices has been shown to reduce stress, improve mood, and enhance overall quality of life.

As we continue to uncover the science behind restorative practices, it becomes increasingly clear that prioritizing rest and relaxation is not just a luxury, it's a necessity for our health and well-being. So let us embrace the power of restorative practices and make time for relaxation and rejuvenation in our lives. For it is through these practices that we can nourish our minds, bodies, and spirits, and cultivate a life of lasting happiness and fulfillment.

## Mindfulness, Meditation, and Quality Sleep

In our fast-paced world, it can be easy to overlook the importance of mindfulness, meditation, and quality sleep in maintaining our overall well-being. However, these practices are essential for cultivating a sense of inner peace, resilience, and vitality in the face of life's challenges. In this chapter, we will explore the benefits of mindfulness, meditation, and quality sleep, and how they can help us master slow productivity for lasting success and well-being.

Mindfulness is the practice of paying attention to the present moment with openness, curiosity, and acceptance. It involves tuning into our thoughts, feelings, and sensations without judgment, and cultivating a greater awareness of our internal and external experiences. Research has shown that mindfulness can reduce stress, anxiety, and depression, and improve overall well-being. By incorporating mindfulness into our daily lives, we can develop greater clarity, focus, and resilience, enabling us to navigate life's challenges with grace and ease.

Meditation is a related practice that involves training the mind to focus and quiet the chatter of our thoughts. There are many different forms of meditation, including mindfulness meditation, loving-kindness meditation, and breath awareness meditation, each with its own unique benefits. Regular meditation practice has been shown to reduce stress, improve concentration, and promote emotional well-being. By carving out time each day for meditation, we can cultivate a greater sense of peace, balance, and inner harmony.

Quality sleep is another essential component of our overall well-being.

During sleep, our bodies undergo a process of repair and regeneration, allowing us to recover from the physical and mental demands of the day. Research has shown that chronic sleep deprivation can have serious consequences for our health, increasing our risk of obesity, diabetes, heart disease, and other chronic illnesses. By prioritizing good sleep hygiene and creating a relaxing bedtime routine, we can improve the quality of our sleep and reap the benefits of a well-rested mind and body.

Incorporating mindfulness, meditation, and quality sleep into our daily lives is not always easy, especially in a culture that values constant productivity and achievement. However, the benefits of these practices are undeniable, and the rewards are well worth the effort. By prioritizing our well-being and making time for rest and relaxation, we can cultivate a more balanced, fulfilling, and sustainable approach to life. So let us embrace the power of mindfulness, meditation, and quality sleep, and harness their transformative potential to master slow productivity for lasting success and well-being.

## Cultivating Mindful Productivity

In our fast-paced world, productivity is often equated with busyness and constant activity. However, there is a growing recognition that true productivity is not about how much we do, but rather about how effectively we use our time and energy. In this chapter, we will explore the concept of mindful productivity and how it can help us master slow productivity for lasting success and well-being.

Mindful productivity involves approaching our tasks and responsibilities with a sense of presence, awareness, and intentionality.

It's about being fully engaged in the present moment, rather than being distracted by thoughts of the past or worries about the future. When we practice mindful productivity, we are able to focus our attention more effectively, make better decisions, and achieve greater satisfaction and fulfillment in our work.

One of the key principles of mindful productivity is the idea of single-tasking. Unlike multitasking, which involves trying to juggle multiple tasks at once, single-tasking involves focusing our attention on one task at a time. Research has shown that multitasking can actually decrease productivity and increase stress, as our brains are not designed to handle multiple tasks simultaneously. By practicing single-tasking, we can improve our focus, reduce our stress levels, and accomplish more in less time.

Another important aspect of mindful productivity is the practice of prioritization. Rather than trying to do everything at once, we must learn to identify the tasks that are most important and focus our energy on those first. This requires us to develop a keen awareness of our goals, priorities, and values, and to align our actions with what truly matters to us. By prioritizing our tasks in this way, we can ensure that we are making the most of our time and energy and that we are focusing on the activities that will have the greatest impact on our success and well-being.

Mindful productivity also involves taking regular breaks and periods of rest throughout the day. Research has shown that taking breaks can actually improve our focus, creativity, and productivity, as it gives our brains time to recharge and reset. By incorporating short breaks into our workday, we can prevent burnout and maintain a sense of balance and equilibrium in our lives.

Ultimately, mindful productivity is about finding the right balance between activity and rest, effort and ease. It's about approaching our tasks and responsibilities with a sense of mindfulness and intentionality, rather than simply going through the motions. By cultivating mindful productivity in our lives, we can achieve greater success and well-being, and live more deeply and fully in every moment.

**Integrating Mindfulness into Daily Routines**

Incorporating mindfulness into our daily routines is essential for cultivating a sense of presence, awareness, and intentionality in our lives. Mindfulness is the practice of paying attention to the present moment with openness, curiosity, and acceptance, and it can be applied to virtually any activity or situation.

One of the simplest ways to integrate mindfulness into our daily routines is through the practice of mindful breathing. By taking a few moments each day to focus on our breath, we can anchor ourselves in the present moment and cultivate a sense of calm and clarity. Mindful breathing can be done anytime, anywhere, and can be especially helpful during times of stress or overwhelm.

Another way to integrate mindfulness into our daily routines is through the practice of mindful eating. Rather than rushing through meals or eating on autopilot, we can take the time to savor each bite, noticing the flavors, textures, and sensations of the food. By bringing our full attention to the act of eating, we can cultivate a greater appreciation for nourishing our bodies and develop healthier eating habits.

Mindfulness can also be integrated into our daily routines through the practice of mindful movement. This can include activities such as yoga, tai chi, or simply going for a walk in nature. By paying attention to the sensations of our bodies as we move, we can cultivate a greater sense of presence and embodiment, and reduce stress and tension in the body and mind.

In addition to these formal practices, mindfulness can also be integrated into our daily routines through informal practices such as mindful listening, mindful communication, and mindful work. By bringing a sense of mindfulness and presence to all of our activities, we can cultivate a greater sense of connection, engagement, and fulfillment in our lives.

## Developing Awareness of Actions and Priorities

Developing awareness of our actions and priorities is essential for cultivating mindful productivity and mastering slow productivity for lasting success and well-being. Awareness is the foundation of mindfulness, and it allows us to bring greater intentionality and purpose to our daily lives.

One of the first steps in developing awareness is to cultivate a sense of presence in the present moment. This involves tuning into our thoughts, feelings, and sensations with curiosity and openness, rather than being caught up in autopilot mode. By bringing awareness to the present moment, we can become more attuned to our thoughts and behaviors, and make more conscious choices about how we spend our time and energy.

Another important aspect of developing awareness is to cultivate a sense of clarity around our priorities and goals. This requires us to take the time to reflect on what truly matters to us and to identify the activities and tasks that align with our values and aspirations. By clarifying our priorities, we can focus our energy on the things that are most important to us, and let go of the things that are not serving us.

Developing awareness also involves cultivating a sense of curiosity and inquiry into our habits and patterns of behavior. This means being willing to question the beliefs and assumptions that drive our actions and explore new ways of thinking and being. By cultivating a spirit of curiosity, we can break free from the constraints of habit and routine, and open ourselves up to new possibilities and opportunities for growth and transformation.

Ultimately, developing awareness of our actions and priorities is a lifelong journey, one that requires patience, practice, and self-reflection. But by cultivating awareness in our daily lives, we can become more intentional and purposeful in our actions, and create a greater sense of meaning and fulfillment in all that we do. So let us embrace the power of awareness, and cultivate mindful productivity for lasting success and well-being.

# Chapter Four: Key Principles of Slow Productivity

In a world that often glorifies busyness and constant activity, the concept of slow productivity offers a refreshing alternative, a way of working and living that prioritizes quality over quantity, intentionality over speed, and sustainability over short-term gains. In this chapter, we will explore the key principles of slow productivity and how they can help us master the gentle pace for lasting success and well-being.

**Principle 1: Prioritization and Focus**

At the heart of slow productivity lies the principle of prioritization and focus. Rather than trying to do everything at once, slow productivity encourages us to identify the tasks and activities that are most important and focus our energy on those first. This requires us to cultivate a deep awareness of our goals, values, and priorities, and to align our actions with what truly matters to us. By prioritizing our tasks in this way, we can ensure that we are making the most of our time and energy and that we are focusing on the activities that will have the greatest impact on our success and well-being.

## Principle 2: Mindful Presence

Another key principle of slow productivity is mindful presence. The practice of being fully engaged in the present moment, with awareness, curiosity, and acceptance. Rather than rushing through our tasks on autopilot, slow productivity encourages us to bring our full attention to whatever we are doing, whether it's work, leisure, or rest. By cultivating a mindful presence in our daily lives, we can develop greater clarity, focus, and resilience, enabling us to navigate life's challenges with grace and ease.

## Principle 3: Balance and Harmony

Balance and harmony are essential principles of slow productivity, as they remind us of the importance of finding equilibrium in all aspects of our lives. Slow productivity encourages us to honor our need for rest, relaxation, and rejuvenation, and to create space for these activities in our daily routines. By balancing our time and energy between work, leisure, and self-care, we can prevent burnout, maintain a sense of well-being, and cultivate a more sustainable approach to productivity.

**Principle 4: Reflection and Iteration**

Reflection and iteration are key components of the slow productivity process, as they allow us to continuously evaluate our goals, strategies, and progress, and make adjustments as needed. Slow productivity encourages us to take regular moments for reflection, whether it's at the end of the day, the week, or the month, to assess what's working well and what could be improved. By incorporating reflection and iteration into our daily lives, we can refine our approach to productivity, learn from our mistakes, and make meaningful progress toward our goals.

**Principle 5: Gratitude and Appreciation**

Finally, slow productivity emphasizes the importance of gratitude and appreciation in our lives. By cultivating a sense of gratitude for the present moment and appreciation for the people and experiences that enrich our lives, we can cultivate a greater sense of happiness, fulfillment, and well-being. Slow productivity encourages us to slow down and savor the simple pleasures of life, whether it's a beautiful sunset, a delicious meal, or a heartfelt conversation with a loved one. By practicing gratitude and appreciation, we can cultivate a deeper sense of connection, meaning, and purpose in our lives.

Incorporating these key principles of slow productivity into our daily lives can help us master the gentle pace and achieve lasting success and well-being. By prioritizing and focusing on what truly matters, cultivating a mindful presence, finding balance and harmony, engaging in regular reflection and iteration, and practicing gratitude and appreciation, we can create a more fulfilling and meaningful life for ourselves and those around us.

## Doing Fewer Things with Greater Intention

In our fast-paced world, it's easy to fall into the trap of trying to do everything at once, juggling multiple tasks, commitments, and responsibilities in an endless pursuit of productivity and achievement. However, the reality is that trying to do too much can actually be counterproductive, leading to stress, overwhelm, and burnout.

## The Myth of Multitasking

One of the biggest myths of productivity is the idea that multitasking is an effective way to get more done in less time. In reality, multitasking can actually decrease productivity and quality of work, as our brains are not designed to handle multiple tasks simultaneously. When we try to do too much at once, we end up spreading ourselves thin, making it difficult to focus our attention and perform at our best. Instead of multitasking, slow productivity encourages us to focus on one task at a time, giving it our full attention and effort.

## The Power of Single-Tasking

Single-tasking, or focusing on one task at a time, is a core principle of slow productivity. By dedicating our full attention and energy to each task, we can achieve greater focus, clarity, and efficiency, leading to higher-quality work and better outcomes. Single-tasking also allows us to fully immerse ourselves in the present moment, rather than being pulled in multiple directions by competing demands. By embracing the power of single-tasking, we can reduce stress, improve our productivity, and experience greater satisfaction and fulfillment in our work.

## The Importance of Prioritization

Doing fewer things with greater intention also involves prioritizing our tasks and activities based on their importance and urgency. Rather than trying to do everything at once, slow productivity encourages us to identify the tasks that are most important and focus our energy on those first. This requires us to cultivate a deep awareness of our goals, values, and priorities, and to align our actions with what truly matters to us. By prioritizing our tasks in this way, we can ensure that we are making the most of our time and energy and that we are focusing on the activities that will have the greatest impact on our success and well-being.

**Creating Space for Reflection and Rest**

In addition to prioritizing our tasks, doing fewer things with greater intention also involves creating space for reflection and rest. Rather than constantly pushing ourselves to do more, slow productivity encourages us to take regular breaks and periods of rest throughout the day. This allows us to recharge our batteries, prevent burnout, and maintain a sense of balance and well-being. By incorporating moments of reflection and rest into our daily routines, we can cultivate a more sustainable approach to productivity and achieve greater success and fulfillment in our lives.

## Working at a Natural Pace

In our modern world, the pressure to work at a breakneck pace can be overwhelming. We're constantly bombarded with messages that tell us to hustle harder, work faster, and never slow down. But the truth is, working at a natural pace, not a frenetic one, is essential for our well-being and long-term success.

## Understanding Your Body's Rhythms

Each of us has a natural rhythm, a unique ebb and flow of energy and focus that fluctuates throughout the day. Some people are naturally more productive in the morning, while others hit their stride in the afternoon or evening. By paying attention to your body's rhythms and honoring your natural energy levels, you can optimize your productivity and work more effectively.

## The Importance of Rest and Recovery

Working at a natural pace also involves recognizing the importance of rest and recovery. Just as our bodies need time to rest and recharge after physical activity, our minds need time to rest and recharge after periods of intense focus and concentration. By taking regular breaks throughout the day and prioritizing restorative activities such as meditation, mindfulness, and leisure, we can prevent burnout, maintain our mental clarity, and sustain our productivity over the long term.

## Embracing Slow Progress

In a culture that values instant gratification and overnight success, it can be tempting to rush through our work and expect immediate results. However, true progress often takes time, sometimes longer than we'd like. Working at a natural pace involves embracing the idea of slow progress, of taking small, incremental steps towards our goals and trusting that each step brings us closer to our desired outcome. By focusing on the process rather than the end result, we can cultivate patience, resilience, and a greater sense of satisfaction in our work.

## Finding Flow

Working at a natural pace also allows us to tap into a state of flow, a state of deep immersion and effortless concentration in our work. Flow occurs when we're fully engaged in a task that challenges us just enough to stretch our abilities, but not so much that it overwhelms us. By creating the right conditions for flow, such as clear goals, immediate feedback, and a balance between challenge and skill, we can enhance our creativity, productivity, and overall well-being.

Incorporating these principles of working at a natural pace into our daily lives can help us master the gentle pace and achieve lasting success and well-being. By understanding our body's rhythms, prioritizing rest and recovery, embracing slow progress, and finding flow in our work, we can create a more sustainable approach to productivity and thrive in all areas of our lives.

## Chapter Five: A More Sustainable Alternative

In a world that often celebrates hustle culture and glorifies busyness, it's easy to get caught up in the relentless pursuit of productivity and achievement. However, this constant pressure to do more, be more, and achieve more can take a toll on our physical, mental, and emotional well-being.

### The Pitfalls of Hustle Culture

Hustle culture is characterized by a relentless focus on productivity, success, and achievement at all costs. It glorifies the idea of "hustling" and "grinding" as badges of honor and encourages people to push themselves to their limits in pursuit of their goals. However, this relentless pursuit of productivity can come at a significant cost to our health and well-being. It can lead to burnout, stress, anxiety, and a sense of overwhelm, as we struggle to keep up with the ever-increasing demands placed upon us.

## The Benefits of a Gentle Pace

In contrast to hustle culture, a gentle pace offers a more sustainable alternative, a way of working and living that prioritizes balance, well-being, and fulfillment. It recognizes that true productivity is not about how much we do, but rather about how effectively we use our time and energy. By embracing a gentle pace, we can cultivate a greater sense of presence, purpose, and meaning in our lives, and achieve greater success and fulfillment in the long run.

## Finding Balance and Harmony

At the heart of a gentle pace lies the principle of balance and harmony. Rather than constantly pushing ourselves to do more, a gentle pace encourages us to find equilibrium in all aspects of our lives, work, leisure, relationships, and self-care. It recognizes that true productivity is not about working harder, but rather about working smarter, prioritizing our tasks, focusing on what truly matters, and creating space for rest and rejuvenation. By finding balance and harmony in our lives, we can prevent burnout, reduce stress, and cultivate a greater sense of well-being and fulfillment.

## Embracing Slow Productivity

Slow productivity is at the core of a gentle pace. It's about approaching our tasks and responsibilities with a sense of mindfulness, intentionality, and purpose, rather than rushing through them on autopilot. Slow productivity encourages us to do fewer things with greater intention, focus, and presence, and to prioritize quality over quantity in all that we do. By embracing slow productivity, we can achieve greater satisfaction and fulfillment in our work, and create a more sustainable approach to productivity that honors our health and well-being.

## Understanding Aimless Overwhelm

Aimless overwhelm occurs when we feel overwhelmed by the sheer volume of tasks and responsibilities in our lives, but lack a clear sense of direction or purpose. It's like spinning our wheels in mud, we're expending a lot of energy, but not making much progress towards our goals. Aimless overwhelm can leave us feeling stuck, frustrated, and exhausted, as we struggle to find meaning and fulfillment in our work and lives.

## Cultivating Clarity and Focus

One of the first steps in overcoming aimless overwhelm is to cultivate clarity and focus in our lives. This involves taking the time to clarify our goals, values, and priorities, and to identify the tasks and activities that align with them. By focusing our energy on what truly matters to us, we can avoid getting bogged down by distractions and busy work, and make meaningful progress towards our goals.

## Setting Boundaries and Saying No

Another important strategy for overcoming aimless overwhelm is to set boundaries and learn to say no to things that don't align with our priorities. This can be challenging, especially in a culture that values constant busyness and productivity. However, setting boundaries is essential for protecting our time and energy, and ensuring that we have the space to focus on what truly matters to us. By learning to say no to things that don't serve us, we can create more time and space for the activities and relationships that bring us joy and fulfillment.

## Creating a Sustainable Routine

Creating a sustainable routine is another key strategy for overcoming aimless overwhelm. This involves establishing daily habits and rituals that support our well-being and productivity, such as setting aside time for self-care, exercise, and relaxation. By incorporating these activities into our daily routines, we can prevent burnout, reduce stress, and cultivate a greater sense of balance and harmony in our lives.

## Step-by-Step Advice for a Slower, More Humane Alternative

Making the shift to a slower, more humane alternative to hustle culture can feel overwhelming at first. It requires us to challenge deeply ingrained beliefs and habits and embrace a new way of working and living that prioritizes balance, well-being, and fulfillment. Here, we will explore step-by-step advice for embracing a slower, more humane alternative and mastering the gentle pace for lasting success and well-being.

### Step 1: Clarify Your Priorities

The first step in embracing a slower, more humane alternative is to clarify your priorities. Take some time to reflect on what truly matters to you, your values, goals, and aspirations, and identify the tasks and activities that align with them. By clarifying your priorities, you can focus your energy on what truly matters to you, and let go of the things that don't serve you.

## Step 2: Set Boundaries and Say No

Once you've clarified your priorities, the next step is to set boundaries and learn to say no to things that don't align with them. This can be challenging, especially if you're used to saying yes to everything that comes your way. However, setting boundaries is essential for protecting your time and energy, and ensuring that you have the space to focus on what truly matters to you.

## Step 3: Establish a Sustainable Routine

Creating a sustainable routine is another important step in embracing a slower, more humane alternative. This involves establishing daily habits and rituals that support your well-being and productivity, such as setting aside time for self-care, exercise, and relaxation. By incorporating these activities into your daily routine, you can prevent burnout, reduce stress, and cultivate a greater sense of balance and harmony in your life.

**Step 4: Practice Mindful Productivity**

Finally, practice mindful productivity by approaching your tasks and responsibilities with a sense of presence, awareness, and intentionality. Rather than rushing through them on autopilot, take the time to focus your attention fully on each task, and give it the care and attention it deserves. By practicing mindful productivity, you can achieve greater satisfaction and fulfillment in your work, and create a more sustainable approach to productivity that honors your health and well-being.

By following these steps, you can embrace a slower, more humane alternative to hustle culture and master the gentle pace for lasting success and well-being. Remember, it's not about doing more, but rather about doing what truly matters with intention, focus, and presence. So take a deep breath, slow down, and embrace the gentle pace of life.

## Sustainable Success and Well-being

Relentless pursuit of success can come at a cost to our well-being, leaving us feeling burnt out, stressed, and unfulfilled.

Sustainable success and well-being go hand in hand, they are two sides of the same coin. True success is not just about achieving external markers of accomplishment, such as wealth, status, or recognition. It's also about feeling fulfilled, content, and at peace with ourselves and our lives. Similarly, well-being is not just about physical health or material comfort. It's also about feeling a sense of purpose, meaning, and connection in our lives.

Sustainable success and well-being require us to take a holistic approach to our lives, one that takes into account not just our professional achievements, but also our personal relationships, physical health, mental well-being, and spiritual fulfillment. It's about finding balance and harmony in all aspects of our lives and cultivating a sense of wholeness and integration that allows us to thrive in all areas.

## The Role of Slow Productivity in Sustainable Success

Slow productivity plays a crucial role in achieving sustainable success and well-being. Unlike traditional approaches to productivity that focus solely on getting more done in less time, slow productivity emphasizes the importance of quality over quantity, presence over speed, and intentionality over busyness. It encourages us to slow down, savor the moment, and focus on what truly matters, rather than getting caught up in the relentless pursuit of productivity and achievement.

By mastering slow productivity, we can create the space and freedom to prioritize our well-being and fulfillment, rather than sacrificing them on the altar of success. We can cultivate a deeper sense of presence and awareness in our lives, enabling us to fully engage with our work, our relationships, and ourselves. We can also develop greater resilience and adaptability, allowing us to navigate life's challenges with grace and ease.

## Practices for Cultivating Sustainable Success and Well-being

Cultivating sustainable success and well-being requires a combination of mindset shifts, daily practices, and intentional actions. Here are some practices to help you cultivate sustainable success and well-being in your own life:

1. **Mindfulness Meditation:** Mindfulness meditation is a

powerful practice for cultivating presence, awareness, and inner peace. By taking a few moments each day to sit quietly and observe your thoughts and sensations without judgment, you can cultivate a greater sense of clarity, focus, and equanimity in your life.

2. **Gratitude Journaling:** Keeping a gratitude journal is a simple yet effective way to cultivate gratitude and appreciation for the abundance in your life. Each day, take a few moments to write down three things you're grateful for, no matter how small or insignificant they may seem. This practice can

help shift your focus from what's lacking to what's already present, fostering a greater sense of contentment and well-being.

3. **Regular Exercise:** Regular exercise is essential for maintaining physical health, but it also has powerful benefits for mental and emotional well-being. Whether it's going for a walk, practicing yoga, or hitting the gym, find a form of exercise that you enjoy and make it a regular part of your routine. Not only will it help you feel better physically, but it can also boost your mood, reduce

stress, and improve your overall quality of life.

4. **Setting Boundaries:** Setting boundaries is essential for protecting your time, energy, and well-being. Learn to say no to things that don't align with your priorities or values, and create space for the activities and relationships that bring you joy and fulfillment. This may mean turning down extra work projects, setting limits on your availability, or prioritizing self-care activities.

5. **Cultivating Essential Meaningful Relationships:** Meaningful relationships are essential for

well-being and fulfillment. Take the time to nurture your relationships with friends, family, and loved ones, and make time for meaningful connection and communication. Whether it's having dinner with a friend, going for a hike with your partner, or simply calling your parents, prioritize quality time with the people who matter most to you.

## Conclusion

In a world that often values achievement over well-being, it's easy to get caught up in the relentless pursuit of success at any cost. However, true success and well-being are not mutually exclusive, they are intrinsically linked, and one cannot be achieved without the other. By embracing slow productivity and cultivating sustainable success and well-being, we can create a more fulfilling and meaningful life for ourselves and those around us. So let us slow down, savor the moment, and embrace the gentle pace of life as we journey towards lasting success and well-being.

www.ingramcontent.com/pod-product-compliance
Lightning Source LLC
Chambersburg PA
CBHW071213240526
45470CB00018B/1853